All Kinds of Friends

My Friend Is Blind

by Kirsten Chang

Bullfrog Books

Ideas for Parents and Teachers

Bullfrog Books let children practice reading informational text at the earliest reading levels. Repetition, familiar words, and photo labels support early readers.

Before Reading

- Discuss the cover photo. What does it tell them?

- Look at the picture glossary together. Read and discuss the words.

Read the Book

- "Walk" through the book and look at the photos. Let the child ask questions. Point out the photo labels.

- Read the book to the child, or have him or her read independently.

After Reading

- Prompt the child to think more. Ask: Do you know someone who is blind? What are some ways you could be a good friend to him or her?

Bullfrog Books are published by Jump!
5357 Penn Avenue South
Minneapolis, MN 55419
www.jumplibrary.com

Library of Congress Cataloging-in-Publication Data

Names: Chang, Kirsten, 1991– author.
Title: My friend is blind / by Kirsten Chang.
Description: Minneapolis, MN: Bullfrog Books, Jump!, Inc., [2020]
Series: All kinds of friends | Includes index.
Identifiers: LCCN 2018048533 (print)
LCCN 2018050963 (ebook)
ISBN 9781641287340 (ebook)
ISBN 9781641287326 (hardcover : alk. paper)
ISBN 9781641287333 (pbk.)
Subjects: LCSH: Blind—Juvenile literature.
Friendship—Juvenile literature.
Classification: LCC HV1593 (ebook)
LCC HV1593 .C45 2020 (print) | DDC 305.9/081—dc23
LC record available at https://lccn.loc.gov/2018048533

Editor: Susanne Bushman
Designer: Molly Ballanger

Photo Credits: Tad Saddoris, cover, 1 (left); aekkom/Shutterstock, 1 (right); andresr/iStock, 3; IvanJekic/iStock, 4, 5, 6–7, 23tr; apixel/iStock, 8, 9, 23br; NurPhoto/Getty, 10–11, 23tl; LuisPortugal/iStock, 12, 22tl; Fuss Sergey/Shutterstock, 12–13; stockfour/Shutterstock, 14–15; warapatrs/Shutterstock, 15; FatCamera/iStock, 16–17; TexPhoto/iStock, 18; ABK/BSIP/Age Fotostock, 19, 23bl; Chatchai Somwat/Dreamstime, 20–21; Julian Rovagnati/Shutterstock, 22tr; Konstantin Shaleev/Shutterstock, 22bl; IrynaL/Shutterstock, 22br; tirc83/iStock, 24.

Printed in the United States of America at Corporate Graphics in North Mankato, Minnesota.

Table of Contents

Good Friends

Lila is my friend.

Glasses help her see.

We play games.
We have fun!

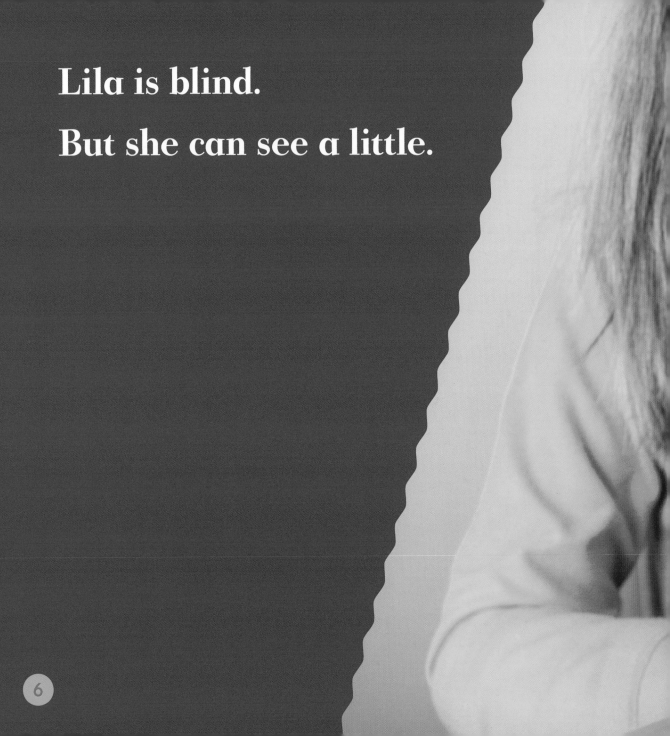

Lila is blind.

But she can see a little.

Champp is her guide dog.
He helps her get around.

guide dog

8

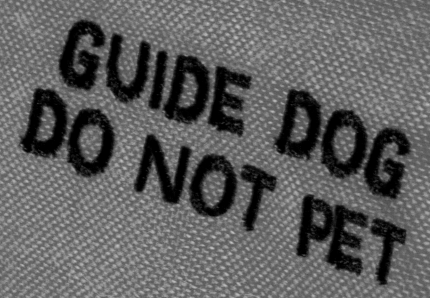

We do not pet Champ.

He is working!

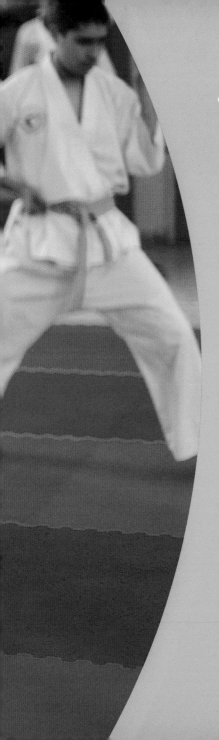

Jade is blind.

She cannot see at all.

She loves to be active!

Todd reads a book to me.

It is in Braille.

The letters are small bumps.

He uses his fingers.

Braille ·····▶

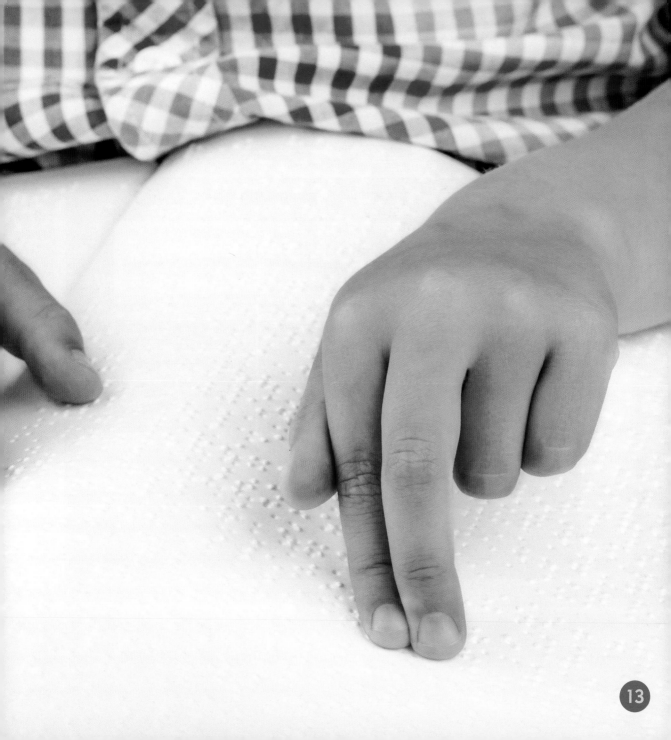

Earth has layers.
The core is the hottest.

He has a tablet, too.

He asks it to read to him.

It helps him learn.

Being blind doesn't
stop Nel.

She sees with one eye.

She goes to school.

She reads.

Nate stops at the crosswalk.

He listens.

Beeps tell him it is safe
to cross.

His cane helps him.
It feels what is
around him.

cane

19

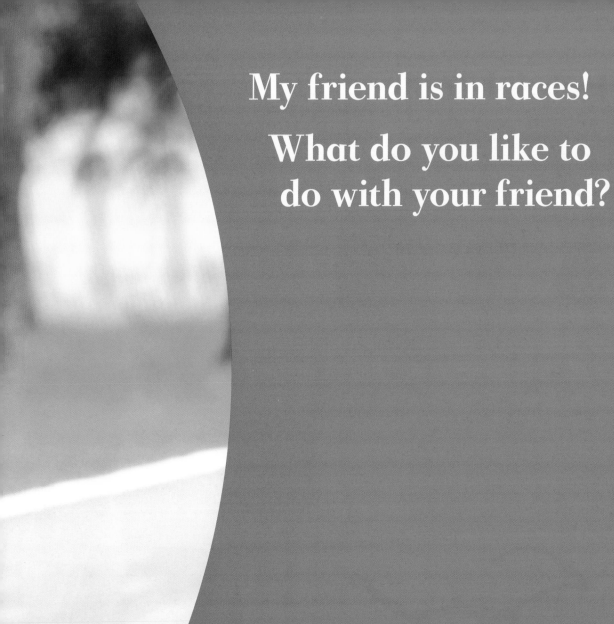

My friend is in races!
What do you like to
do with your friend?

Helpful Tools

Braille
Braille uses small raised dots in place of letters. People who are blind read by feeling the dots.

cane
Canes help people who are blind feel what is around them.

glasses
Glasses are two pieces of specially cut glass or plastic in a frame that help people see more clearly.

tablet
Special tablets read text aloud so that people who are blind can use them.

Picture Glossary

active
Participating in physical activity.

blind
Not able to see or only able to see very little.

crosswalk
A place where people cross the street.

guide dog
A dog trained to lead a person who is blind.

Index

To Learn More

FACT SURFER

Finding more information is as easy as 1, 2, 3.

❶ Go to www.factsurfer.com

❷ Enter "myfriendisblind" into the search box.

❸ Choose your book to see a list of websites.